Feet of the Messenger

Encountering these poems you might think of B. H. Fairchild, James Wright, Gary Snyder, Brian Turner, but you'd be wrong. This is original work where time jumps, as does the boundary betwixt reality and dream, memory and imagination. And war, as it will, soaks all. H. C. Palmer writes with the visceral authority of combat seen and visions earned. Vital, necessary reading . . .

—Donald Anderson, *Fire Road* and *Gathering Noise from My Life: A Camouflaged Memoir*

As a young medical resident, H. C. Palmer was drafted by Lyndon Baines Johnson to serve in the Vietnam War. He treated comrades and wounded civilians alike; he saw many die. In *Feet of the Messenger*, he has produced an extraordinary testament to that moment in history and to its afterlife. America did not invent the practice of shipping its young people off to slaughter other people on specious pretexts, and H. C. Palmer is far too wise, and far too good a poet, to lecture us on the consequences, but in his tributes to the dead, his tributes to survival, his luminous portraits of compassion and reprieve, he grants us a vision of the better world we still, please heaven, might have a chance to make.

—Linda Gregerson, *Magnetic North* and *Waterborne*

H. C. Palmer's poems evoke a place and a time, Vietnam during the war, with clarity and heart. They are invocations to the spirits of memory and healing. They are witnesses that must be heard.

—Karl Marlantes, *Matterhorn: A Novel of the Vietnam War* and *What It Is Like to Go to War*

Poems

Feet of the Messenger

H. C. PALMER

Afterword by Rhina P. Espaillat

 BkMk Press
University of Missouri-Kansas City
www.umkc.edu/bkmk

BkMk Press
University of Missouri-Kansas City
5101 Rockhill Road
Kansas City, MO 64110
www.umkc.edu/bkmk

Executive Editor: Robert Stewart
Managing Editor: Ben Furnish
Assistant Managing Editor, book design: Cynthia Beard
Associate Editor: Michelle Boisseau
Editorial Consultant: Karen I. Johnson
Cover photo: Cynthia Beard
Vietnamese language consultation: Hang Le

BkMk Press wishes to thank Serena Dobson, Barbara Magiera,
McKensie Callahan, Josiah Pabst, Rebecca Adams, and Megan Schwindler.

Missouri Arts Council
The State of the Arts

Financial support for this project has been provided by
the Missouri Arts Council, a state agency.

BkMk Press also thanks the Miller-Mellor Foundation for its support.

Library of Congress Cataloging-in-Publication Data

Names: Palmer, H. C., 1936- author.
Title: The feet of the messenger / H.C. Palmer.
Description: Kansas City, Missouri : BkMk Press/University of
Missouri-Kansas
   City, 2017. | Includes bibliographical references and index.
Identifiers: LCCN 2017023681 | ISBN 9781943491100 (alk. paper)
Subjects: LCSH: Vietnam War, 1961-1975--Poetry. | Medical care--Poetry. |
   United States. Army--Surgeons--Poetry. | Flint Hills (Kan. and
   Okla.)--Poetry. | Kansas--Poetry.
Classification: LCC PS3616.A33894 A6 2017 | DDC 811/.6--dc23 LC
record available at https://lccn.loc.gov/2017023681

ISBN: 978-1-943491-10-0

How beautiful upon the mountains
are the feet of the messenger
who announces peace.
—Bible, NRSV, Isaiah 52:7

How beautiful on the mountains,
are the feet of the messenger of good tidings,
that announces peace.
—Tanakh, Isaiah 52:7

Contents

III

Acknowledgments

In April 1964, I was one of 1,500 doctors drafted by President Lyndon Johnson from medical-residency-training programs across the United States. None of us suspected we would be going to war. Four months later, Johnson and Defense Secretary Robert McNamara contrived the Gulf of Tonkin Incident and ramped up what had been a discreet but steady invasion and occupation of South Vietnam. By August 1965, I was a battalion surgeon for the First Infantry Division, treating wounded and dying American soldiers and Vietnamese civilian casualties.

In July 1966, after my discharge from the Army, I resumed my residency training at the University of Kansas Medical Center. That first morning back, Dr. Mahlon Delp, chair of internal medicine, asked me to stop by his office. I sat facing him, across his desk. Behind him, on the wall above his credenza, were diplomas, certificates, and photographs. One photograph, dated "77th Evac Hosp./Jan-1945" was of Colonel Delp in front of his hospital tent during the Battle of the Bulge. In the picture, he looked determined but tired.

"Are you okay, H. C.?" he asked. "Sure," I said. "I'm just fine."

Thirty years later I decided to write fly-fishing stories. I was surprised when a Vietnam veteran appeared in the first story I wrote. As I continued to write stories, and for the past ten years, poems, that veteran kept coming back. All those years, I'd packed him away, so to speak, without any conscious intent to do so. After a time, I understood that the American War in Vietnam had changed my life in almost every way—even the way I interpreted memories of childhood.

A year ago, as I was writing an essay about Dr. Delp, I remembered his question and my impulsive answer. I regret I never considered that he was giving me permission to tell him my story and asking if I'd like to listen to his.

A special thanks to Trish Reeves, R. Lanny Hunter, Nick Lyons, Maryfrances Wagner, Greg Field, James Cherry, Robert Stewart, Ben Furnish, Cynthia Beard, and my classroom teachers, Michelle Boisseau, Michael Johnson, and Violet Randolph.

Grateful acknowledgement is made to the following publications in which these poems first appeared, sometimes in slightly different forms or titles:

New Letters: "Selected Notes on Beauty" and "Five Notes from War," both of which were nominated for a Pushcart Prize.

Poetry Daily: "Five Notes from War"

Narrative Magazine: "*If I Die in a Combat Zone*" and "Thompson's Boots."

War, Literature & the Arts: "*Dulce et Decorum Est*: Again," formerly titled "A History Lesson at the Vietnam Veterans Memorial"; "Thompson's Prayer," formerly titled "*Happy Ending*"; "Thơ Hòa Bình"; "A Season for War"; "Break Room at the Ammo Plant"; and "Resurrection."

New Mexico Poetry Review: "Counting Boys in a Truck," "Ode to the Rio Grande Cutthroat," "Great Blue Heron Forgets That Danger Comes from Above and I Forget She's Just a Bird," "Last Hunt," "Considering a Landscape," "In Search of Place," and "The Why Talk."

Flint Hills Review: "Sunset at Lower Fox Creek School," formerly titled "Finding Peace at Lower Fox Creek School."

The Flint Hills: Artistic Impressions of a Tallgrass Prairie (DC Art Press): "The Work of Turkey Vultures," "After Driving Cattle in the Flint Hills," "Elegy for a Prairie Town," "It Was the Wind," "Relecting on This Stone Wall," and "Crow Speaks His Mind After News of *Shock and Awe*."

I-70 Review: "Belated Notes to Mother" (2, 3 and 4) and "Dying to Caruso."

In addition: "Crow Speaks His Mind After News of *Shock and Awe*" and "The Work of Turkey Vultures" were included in *Wildbranch: An Anthology of Nature, Environmental and Place-based Writing* (Utah UP). "Counting Boys in a Truck" was included in *The Whirlybird Anthology of Kansas City Writers.*

*For my wife, Valerie, my children and grandchildren,
and "Men of October 1965"*

I

. . . memory is capricious. It ambushed me when I least expected it and deserted me when I needed it most.

—R. Lanny Hunter

Aristotle's notion that history accretes but only poetry unifies is a notion worth subscribing to.

—Donald Anderson

Bird-Hunting the Tall Grass

Shot at close range
the little hen has come
apart. Her feathers,
wet with her blood,
cling to my fingers.

I probe the femoral artery
where fragments
of the sergeant's fatigues
penetrate the wound.
After it's over
and for a long time,
I pick at my fingers—
threads in congealed blood.

On my knees,
beside the spring
creek, I wash
the feathers away.

If I Die in a Combat Zone

If I must be killed,
I wish to be killed by a sniper.

His efficient nail
does not require a tree

or an IED. I want to be remembered
magnified, lit up,

hanging on his crosshairs.
I want him to believe

he might have loved me
in a different war.

A Season for War

They had overcome him in the end, tenaciously . . .
taking him down. Their heavy shots splashed into him . . .
with that courageous passion peculiar to hunters.
—James Salter

Billy and I potshot what we mistook for a duck
back in 7th grade at Santa Fe Lake in Neosho County.
The bird dove, surfaced for air, dove and surfaced again,
forced down by salvos of #6 bird shot until it floated

and washed to shore. I presented the bird to my father
like a sinner's offering and remember saying,
If it had flown, it might have lived. A loon, he said
without taking it. *They don't often range in Kansas*

and they're never in season. Last time I saw Billy was Đà Nẵng.
A forward air controller flying O-1E Bird Dogs, he marked
VC positions with the bright smoke of white phosphorus rockets.
I flew one mission. Rode the tandem seat. We packed M16s.

He controlled the aircraft by working the stick with his knees—
hands free to fire through pop-open windows. 2 sampans,
ferrying Vietnamese dressed in black, motored across
the Hán River. *Shoot 'em,* he said through my headset.

Ducks on a pond. I aimed far to the side. That night,
at the Oceanside Bar, between chugs of Tiger Beer, Billy teased,
You're still a lousy shot, Doctor. Billy stayed another tour,
rigged an M60 machine gun in place of the tandem seat—

converted his observation plane into attack aircraft.
By tilting or turning, it became a lethal weapon
until diving within range of an AK-47, when Billy took a round
in his chest. He radioed for escort. Huey gunship pilots

called through their mics, *You're losing altitude, Captain,
head for the sea.* Billy and his O-1E splashed on the surf,
rode the breakers upright until lifted onto China Beach,
an open spread of sand as fine and white as altar cloth.

Counting Boys in a Truck

Phước Vĩnh, Vietnam 1965, our first body count

The big deuce-&-a-half
skids to a stop,
nearly clipping a row
of rubber trees
inside our Michelin
plantation firebase.
In the cargo bed
a tangle of arms & legs—
yellow roots torn
from their sandy,
red soil.
We unload 14 bodies
side-by-side—
display 10 AK-47s,
10 bandoliers of 7.62
& 2 60mm mortars
in front of the dead.
The Captain invites
the press—inspects
his night's work.
Fourteen black shirts, he says.
They're all Viet Cong.
I count for myself—
6 wear loincloths,
6 long pants
& 2 naked below their waists
without pubic hair.
I take shots with my 35mm.

Thompson's Prayer

In 1996, Newsweek *magazine named the Rooftop Garden at the Hotel Rex in Ho Chi Minh City as one of one thousand places to visit before you die.*

Two weeks before his death, Thompson
says the name to the cyclo driver,
The Rooftop Garden at the Hotel Rex

& the pith-helmeted old man sings,
Numba' one café in Saigon.
Seventy-five cent lobsters & Pouilly-Fuissé.

Saigon River sampans rock in their moorings,
reflections from red and yellow lanterns stir
the water like goofy carnival rides

& across 50 kilometers—to the edge
of tonight's world, arcs of tracers
& pops of flares & muzzle flashes

from 155s, & a few klicks south,
a progression of fiery billows,
precise as garden rows—750 pound

night blossoms, planted from B-52s,
& two bites later, the rumbles—
the quiver of wine in our glasses.

Thompson says I appear yellow in the light
of the candles. He sucks his fingers—
butter and lemon from his fourth lobster tail,

Surreal shit, man, he says, then presses
his napkin to his lips, *I have a feeling
we should get on a plane and go home.*

After flaming desserts, we walk
to a massage place on Tu Do Street.
not for sex, we say—just to be touched

by a girl. In a room with blackboards
on the walls, mattresses on the floor
& sheets suspended from clotheslines

for privacy, I hear everything.
Thompson is praying, *Jesus* & *Oh my God,*
& the earth rumbles again.

Thompson's Boots

. . . God is surely
patiently trying to immerse us
in a different language
—Denise Levertov

Five klicks south of Phước Vĩnh, Val at my side and my first visit
since the war, I'm searching the old firebase—grown back to jungle
after thirty years—thinking of Thompson the morning he returned
from R & R in Hong Kong, boasting he'd slept with five women in
three different languages. I'm looking for the spot where I'd found
his boots that next morning after the sapper attack—Thompson
vaporized by the satchel charge, except his feet and ankles still inside
the boots—his olive-drab cotton socks turned to secure the laces—
the right boot upright and the left on its side inches away and I
remember how carefully I had lifted them, one in each hand, and
placed them inside a body bag with someone else's body already
there. I remember that zipping sound before we loaded the bag
alongside the two wounded on a Huey dustoff bound for Tân Sơn
Nhất Airbase, and I'm recalling—distinctly now—his socks, the
inked initials, the splashes of blood, and jutting above the socks,
what was left of the shafts of his tibias glistening like the whitest of
ivories, and not two paces away, my landmark, a section of blown
tank track I've just uncovered from the thick vegetation—it must
be that piece of track—twenty four inches square—but rusted, so
when I lift an edge it crumbles, orange residue in my hands, sifting
through my fingers back to earth. Confident now we are near the
exact spot, I reach to touch Val's hand to turn her face from a shaft
of sunlight, then kneel and place her hand on my shoulder, then
my hands where Thompson's boots might have been. I search the
green-mossed undergrowth with my fingertips. It has the texture
of embroidered cloth. I want to pray but don't find the words—and
after a long silence, when I look up, Val is still here.

Thơ Hòa Bình

Trying to rule the world with force
I see this is not succeeding
    —Lao-tzu

It won't hurt you. It's just to kill plants.
    —Karl Marlantes

The *Cô* who cleans our sick-call tent is missing
two days and returns in great pain, her baby
trapped inside her belly, the village midwife
unable to save it. Every breath a siren. We move
her onto a table, where between contractions,
I rotate the head with my hand, but can't
turn it back on course. There is the aroma
of decay and I am making things worse—
the baby's scalp is peeling pulp.

Late afternoon, in the surgical tent, her child
in her arms and wrapped in a bamboo mat,
the *Cô* is chanting—inflected notes with
sharpened edges. The interpreter says,
She sing, baby name Thơ Hòa Bình,
to honor ancestors. She sing, Americans kill
baby from airplane, same way they kill trees
and grandmother. The interpreter says,
She want you remember always,
Thơ Hòa Bình mean Poem of Peace.

dialogue story

While Preparing Separation Documents

Travis Air Force Base, July 1966

The Lieutenant loaded
his Smith-Corona,
typed in blank spaces
on my form DD214.
Fuh king gooks my ass.
Single-fingered key stabs,
metranomed each syllable,
*Fuh king John son's
the prob lem.*
He ripped my papers
from the carriage,
tugged the carbons,
hesitated, then let
his breath go—
like he was
exhausted, or maybe
he'd lost hope.
Oh, Captain,
he waggled my copy,
One more thing.
*If you leave the base
tonight, wear civvies
or be prepared
to wipe spit.*

Five Notes from War

And the hapless Soldier's sigh
Runs in blood down Palace walls
           —William Blake

1.

The lieutenant bled out—
eleven units of plasma
& my friend holding
pressure not enough
to save him.
Near the end
my friend believed
he was transporting
to afterlife when
his fingers trapped
inside the lieutenant's
congealed blood.
We soaked them free
with water
from canteens.
Now, when we visit
The Wall, my friend
tries to wedge
his fingers back in.

2.

Names of the lieutenant & five
more killed that day chiseled
into granite. With fingers spread
& thumbs touching at the tips,
my friend can cover all six
names in chronological order.
Now that we're older, I kneel
behind to steady his forearms.

3.

Last winter, at The Wall
again. Snowing & very cold.
It seemed we were alone
until a man & woman reflected
in the granite from behind us.
For a long time I watched
them inside the stone.
When I turned
I saw them weeping.
Do you have someone here? I asked.
Just the two of you, she said.

4.

A helicopter crash near Bến Cát.
Ed Lehnhoff, the Huey gunship pilot,
the only survivor. Last week
he was arrested for chiseling
The Wall next to the names
of his crewmembers.
The *Washington Post* wrote,
"Mr. Lehnhoff was taken into
custody as he was defacing
the Vietnam Memorial Wall
with a mason's chisel.
Fortunately,
park rangers arrested
him after he carved
just one letter."
Eventually,
after correspondence
from the crew's families,
the Park Service determined
to leave the chiseled "L"
on the right margin
of panel 30E, line 16.

5.

The handsome medic
from Southern California
was straddling our trench latrine
& singing a Beach Boys song
when shot by a Viet Cong sniper.
A high-velocity bullet behind
his right ear. Cranium & contents,
facial bones—vaporized. Half a scalp
of blond hair, eyebrows, eyelashes,
nose & lips—intact.
Ask yourself,
What could a battlefield surgeon do?
I was thinking *funeral.*
How to reconstruct his face.
One last look at sunshine beauty.
I was thinking *Michelangelo*
as I worked inside the cavity
to replicate nasal bones,
cheekbones, forehead, a smile,
until suddenly ashamed
& with a nation's shit on my hands
I heard myself singing,
Wouldn't it be nice if we were older...

Break Room at the Ammo Plant

She works the swing shift
packing 5.56s, believing
one of her bullets—
a single round—will save his life.
In the break room, she's drinking
stale coffee as TV news scrolls
The Names of the Dead—
a squeeze of her cup handle returning
fire when each name slides by.
He's killing those crazy people
with my bullets.

His letters come two or three at a time.
She tips sand from the envelopes
into the lead crystal ashtray
she reserves for special guests.
Saturdays, at the Cherry Street Bar,
wearing perfume of WD-40
& black powder—
she caresses glasses of Boodles
with oil-stained fingers, until
the bartender calls for a cab.

Today, at coffee break, TV news
of a house raid in Fallujah.
Warning, the announcer said.
These images may be disturbing.
In the video, as if flung
against a wall
in a dust-dimmed room
& lit by camera lights,

a mother, her baby,
& a teenage girl—
white blouse, pleated skirt,
& blue hijab—her school books
still wrapped with a cord.

Resurrection

For Sergeant Bales

So Billy uncorked it with his thumbs. It didn't make a pop.
The champagne was dead. So it goes.
—Kurt Vonnegut

In the after-silence, lit by a smoke-filled cone of tactical light, the spent 5.56 caliber metal-cased bullet ascends from the dirt floor, angles for the stone wall, ricochets, then accelerates for the shattered skull of a child fallen into her gush of blood. The bullet unravels her dark hair, restores a pencil-shaped column of blood, brain and fragments of bone, plunges it through her exit wound, seals the tear on her forehead then spirals into the muzzle of the sergeant's M4.

The girl returns to sleep. The sergeant leaps backward through a door as it crashes shut and locks. He back-trails to his basecamp, removes the bullet from his weapon and places it in an ammo canister. He doesn't sleep. At last light he replaces the canister inside a wooden crate at *ammo supply.*

Six weeks earlier, two airmen return the crate to a deuce-and-a-half truck and drive in reverse to an airbase where they ramp the container into a C-17 transport. Negative jet thrust sucks the C-17 onto a runway and airborne to Dover Air Base, USA, where Pentagon contractors carry the container onto a tractor-trailer and drive backward to an ammo factory in Independence, Missouri. A journeyman returns the canister to a workbench. A specialist disassembles the cartridge, smelts the brass to chemical elements.

About the time of the smelting, the American soldier backtracks from a C-130 to a ready room in a hangar at Fort Lewis, Washington, where he warns his commanding officer his life is a mess and might *lose control and do something bad* if he deploys for a fifth tour—this time to a war in Afghanistan, where, on that very day, the girl and her mother rejoice because Americans drove away the Taliban. It is safe to go back to school.

In the Bread Aisle in Safeway

For Larry Colburn

And then, something happens, as you knew it would.
And nothing can ever be the same again.
—Graham Greene

The lieutenant came home from the war carrying visions and echoes and recurring dreams, his soul trashed in a tiny bin of brain, a narrative encrypted in prefrontal snarls and no way to sort it out.

There were playbacks—the worst, the ambush—AK-47s from inside the village, his rifle squad clawing to cover in the shallow road ditch. 7.65s splashing red dirt in their faces, tracers whining overhead and beside and between. *Hold fire,* he ordered, *unless you have a clear shot.* Every villager a hostage and shield. Every hooch a place to hide. Muzzle flashes from windows and doors. Chickens airborne, flailing for rooftops like confetti shot from Fourth of July cannons. And pigs, the damned, squealing pigs, back and forth between the ditch and the village. No way out. Two of his squad down—one dead. There was no choice. *Kill everyone and everything.*

They walked in—the only sounds stifled sobs and thumps of boots against dead pigs. The lieutenant turned to search a pathway between hooches. He saw a woman—so close he heard her breath. She wore black peasant clothes and held a child to her chest. In the woman's free hand an AK-47. The small girl whined, her eyes fixed on his. She made a little cry. The woman raised the muzzle. The lieutenant fired first—through the girl and into the woman's chest.

This morning the woman is back—black blouse and slacks—in the bread aisle at Safeway. She has caged the girl inside a grocery cart. He must act. The woman shoves him away then runs, pushing her cart for the exit. The squeals of those damned pigs rise from the cart's wheels. The girl's cry rising like the shriek of a ghost.

Considering a Landscape

On approach to Memphis, my window frames
fields of rice, a flooded patchwork of angles
& curls lit by the pre-dawn light—
irrigation ditches & canals, east-flowing connections

to the big Mississippi, meandering its way to the Gulf.
The passenger next to me is stowing his computer.
He's forty or so. I say, *These rice farms look just like
the Mekong River Delta*, & he says, *Like what?*

& I say, *You know, those damn rice paddies in Vietnam.*
We pause our descent about 5,000 feet above ground,
a flight level considered safe from small arms fire & I swear,
I hear rotor slaps & feel rotor wash against my face.

I'm strapped at the door of a Huey again—
trembling & sweating & cold. I grab an airsick bag.
C'mon man, he says. *It's thirty years since that war.
You should be over it by now.*

Finding Work After War

Our sons join the army to get work being shot at.
—Jim Harrison

For a long time there were simultaneous
wars, so work was good. Now the wars
are winding down and our poor
are unemployed. They phone
government hotlines then get disconnected.
I know a stonemason disabled from battling
his chisel. He says there will always be his kind
of work—thousands of gravestones
stockpiled in the quarries of Vermont.
He says he's willing to teach,
but worries some might inscribe their own names
before praying into the muzzle of a Colt .45.

Dulce et Decorum Est: Again

(A history lesson at the Vietnam Veterans Memorial)
*In 1913, Ho Chi Minh studied to be a pastry chef
under the French master Escoffier.*

In the hour
before dawn,
the snowflakes
are as fine
as pastry flour.
But with first
cold light, when
they fall large
& heavy on
my hands,
when they cover
the land white
and this Wall
is the dark knife-
edge of my grief—
I understand
it will snow
forever—
bitter *glacés*
sieved through
the old pastry chef's
iron fingers—
his *dessert*
to the main course
gorged at blood-
stained tables
when we trashed
his French *cafés*

and scavenged the spoils
of colonial retreat.
I breathe over a name.
The inscription blurs—
but only for a moment.
I walk panel to panel,
speak the names
over the names
on this *carte d'ardoise*—
as if I could order
them back to life.

Selected Notes on Beauty

And she says, what are you thinking? And I say, beauty.
—B. H. Fairchild

*I did not come here only to grieve
For my people's defeat.*
—James Wright

I.

December 14, 2010, VA Hospital,
Kansas City, Missouri

Back from his tour in Afghanistan, the soldier says,
*Half my foot is gone, Doc, but I'm still in the Guard—
a peacetime soldier now.* I take his foot, a stub
grafted at the arch, trace the spongy edges with my fingers.
No feeling, he laughs. *Beautiful
work, don't you think?*

II.

June 7, 1942, Eastern slope, the Flint Hills, Kansas

One hour past dawn. My father steers our black '36 Pontiac
across a bridge over Buckeye Creek where he stops
at the kill. *The doe will leave only her bones,* he says. I believe
this is good, but worry what I would leave if turkey vultures
fed on me. Buttons? My St. Christopher medal? We drive
from the smell of it, beyond the creek bottom and big cottonwoods
to the top of an incline and a tallgrass prairie where I consider
for the first time what makes something *beautiful*:
hills emerging from deep shadows—sun-brightened tops,
treeless and leveled as if worked by father's carpenter's plane;
early summer bluestem rustling at my knees and a sky so big
I sense a loneliness—like a presence at the Creation. *It's beautiful,*
I say, and he says, *Yes, more beauty than we can take in.*

III.

August 23, 1965, Phước Vĩnh, Vietnam

I'm astonished by a lucid conversation with an infantryman
cradling a bullet inside his brain. *I'm going home to Montana,
Doc. The Madison River Valley.* He tells of a 24-inch rainbow
that holds downstream from Varney Bridge, tucked under
an overhang inside the mouth of Blaine Spring Creek—
describes his fish's transcendent colors as we load him into
a dustoff for Tân Sơn Nhất Hospital. *You don't know what
you're missin', Doc. The most beautiful place in the world.*

IV.

February 8, 1966, Bîen Hòa, Vietnam

Near the airbase, wreckage of a Chinook carrying drums
of jet fuel cracks apart like a spent fire log. Its great rotors
spear the earth. One of the crew props against burned-out
cargo like a boxer, dukes up and ready to strike. When we go
to him he is smiling, the *beautiful* full-toothed grin of incomplete
incineration—ears, nose and lips burned away, eye sockets empty.
Sunlight flashes through breaks in smoke, sparkling his dog tags
like a secret code. I dig at the char with my fingers,
pry a tag's crusted edges to read—

Landfair, Alec B,
US 47 645 572,
O POS,
Protestant

I break his bead-chain, take the tag, and thread it between my own.

V.

September 3, 1993, on Varney Bridge, Montana

In town, news my soldier died at an Army hospital in the Philippines.
A waitress at Ennis Cafe introduced me to his cousin who stands
with me now. He remembers the rainbow and was with my soldier
when he caught the fish *on a size 18 Pale Morning Dun.*
He eases a metal box from his vest pocket. Snaps it open.
Replicas of mayflies, columns hooked across white foam liners.
These are his PMDs, he says. *Real mayflies are ephemeral
but these beauties will last forever.* He closes the box,
then opens it, *On second thought Doc, take one.*

VI.

September 12, 1996, the Vietnam Memorial,
Washington, DC

I place Landfair's dog tag on the pedestal below the panel
inscribed with his name. His tag slides easily under
my finger, the granite's blackness soft as skin.
The stone reflects a *kind of terrible beauty*—
a clear message and no smiles.
Oh, I want to say,
I had nothing to do with it.
I was not here.
I was not born.

VII.

December 14, 2010, the VA, continued

He tells me his boot was blown off by an RPG.
They were isolated five days in a valley called Korengal,
no LZ for a med evac so the medic dressed his wound
then commandeered a boot from a body bag,
searching four bags for one that fit. *That boot*
smelled of rotten flesh but was a gift from Heaven.
That and a little morphine let me stand to fight.
I take his good foot, compare side to side, before
and after, recalling a scripture, *Perhaps these feet.*
He asks, *What do you mean?* and I say *Isaiah—*
it was Isaiah who said, How beautiful upon the mountains
are the feet of the messenger who announces peace.

II

*The mercy of the world is you don't know
what's going to happen.*

—Wendell Berry

Belated Notes to Mother

1. The Milk Barn

After barn chores and supper, after dishes and radio news
from the war, after you read the bedtime story, you printed words
across my back with a fingertip softened by Udder Balm.

Each night a new word—retraced and redefined
until I fell asleep. *Soon this world will be a better place,*
you promised. *One day you can use these words to tell your story.*

Some nights you would sing the words as your finger
swept over my skin like a conductor's baton.
Some nights I asked for a word from the night before—

nights I couldn't get the art of milking out of my mind—
the placement of the wooden stool,
how you kneaded the udder to let down the milk,

your forehead against the cow's flank,
how you played the milk-streams against the tin pail—
the rhythms, the music of froth and cymbal.

2. My Short Love Affair with Venus de Milo

I was 13 when you discovered the photograph, a clip
from *Life* hidden in my stack of T-shirts.
When you unfolded the page, the creases came apart.

She's damaged goods, you said. *And marble is so cold.*
You led me into your bedroom, the corner chair, closed
the door, said, *Watch closely. Don't say a word.*
Back-lit by the room's only window you removed
your clothes as if I wasn't there, lifted your arms
like a ballerina (you later told me 5th position)

and turned once around. You were strong enough
to take me down and I was fearful you would do it.
But you dressed quickly, away from the window,

stepped back into the light, and reached out to me,
as for a small child.

3. The Finals

AAU champion swimmer and diver dies at 86.
  —The Kansas City Star

I woke to sounds of water—inspirations
gulped at intervals between silences
and the night's rain diminishing like the end

of applause. The hospital sheet kicked to the foot
of the bed, blue floral gown (still secure around
your neck), flung over the bedrail like a cape trailing

great momentum—once again naked,
a fetal bird tucked in a cloud of egg crate.
It was like Micki King's Olympic comeback—

when we watched the finals in '72—you lifted
from the springboard, measured your space,
then released your breath on entry.

4. Daffodils

Early this morning I searched your garden
to find a yellow flower for the Mass
and found your daffodils overrun—

wreckage of a night's killing frost.
I thought to bring a single stem—
some confirmation—

but there was such sorrow
in that littered field, leaves unraveling
like ragged burlap shrouds.

Long ago, I believed you would live forever.
Now your daffodils are gone—
but only for a season.

Dying to Caruso

Laugh, clown, at your broken love…
at the pain that poisons your heart
— Ruggero Leoncavallo

Nonno lost his right side to a stroke.
No more kneading the dough or sliding the peel,
his Italian bakery closed for good. No more
Mangia e statti zitto or calling me *Boy.*

On weekends, I played Caruso from a spring-powered
Victrola at his bedside, intensified volume
by opening horn-doors on the mahogany console
while he lip-synched, impassioned,

Ridi Pagliaccio, sul tuo amore in franto! The words
were not perfectly shaped, but with a casual look,
a stranger might believe he was Maestro himself.
I was seven. There were no secrets.

A Cardinal's anointing could not protect the old man
from reprisals. I never considered he was lip-synching
his last confession, believing God would disregard
the lyrics when He heard the impeccable high C.

Ode to the Rio Grande Cutthroat

Oncorhynchus clarki virginalis

O. clarki virginalis
New Mexican original
reduced to remnant
in Rio San Jose's refuge,
you are the treasure flashing
in sunlit high-country pools.
Survivor of civilizations,
you are nature's fine jeweler—
turquoise flanks and silver belly.
You hold secrets
in your amethystine eyes.
You celebrate the big cat, too—
long ago exiled to Mexico—
with a cloisonné
the jaguar motif at your tail.
Before Coronado recorded
your existence, before people
of Pueblo, Folsom and Clovis,
before Sapiens explored
Rio Grande's gorges
and headwater meadows,
when Great Spirit blood-washed
the Sangre de Cristos,
she brushed your throat—
marked you her own.

The Dead in Photographs

On my desk
& bookshelves
are twenty or so
photographs
from war & writing,
school & doctoring—
two of us,
sometimes three,
pressing shoulders,
surely happy
to be there,
together.
Now, we are dying.
To update, I'd
need scissors
& a steady hand.
But that would
leave cutouts—
or you could say
templates—
& templates
are for duplication,
something I don't wish
to encourage.

Death of a Soldier

Jest roll to your rifle and blow out your brains
An' go to your Gawd like a soldier
—Rudyard Kipling

For Cornelius Clark, 5th Special Forces:
Camp Plei Me survivor, October 1965.
Died of pancreatic cancer at age 68.

Surgeons attacked the obstruction, in theory
a tactical move to outflank the tumor.
Techs fired protons at his pancreas, nearly
piercing his heart—a mop-up maneuver.
At treatment stations, IVs filled his veins
with chemo and vitamins—a remedial blast.
For months he chilled and retched and strained,
advanced and retreated until at last
home, his children took his hand, tried to conjure
the young soldier, but startled by bitter breath
and yellow eyes, could not speak, unsure
words could overcome the stench of death.
Battlefields, he said, *never dignify.*
I'm tired of people watching me die.

Death of a Dead Person

For Terri Schiavo

For while we are in this tent, we groan. . .
for the house not made with hands . . .
　　　　　　—St. Paul

The scan showed a collection
of fluid filled my skull.
A sliver of cortex was all I had
to work with.
Science said I was dead.
But you construed my *dancing eyes*
as responses, my guttural
breaths as communication,
your stubborn denial as a kind of hope.
I could not be resuscitated—
or resurrected
in our conception of time.
But I forgive you.
You didn't understand
I was groaning inside my tent,
longing to be unburdened.

The Why Talk

No one had forecast the hard freeze—an attack swift
and brutal. Even the trees weren't ready for it—

the fifteen degrees. *Formed inside living cells,* she says,
ice crystals can be lethal. She treats cancer patients—

understands stages, prognoses, dying, and surprises—
like this morning. The big red maple dropped

its darkest leaves. The pin oak's leaves, browned and creped
for days, held tight for spring.

The white ash seems unscathed—a tint of gold as before—
until sunup, when the wind squalls from the east,

wrenching branches, shuddering limbs and leaf-stems.
In two hours every single leaf is gone. We watch

the shedding through the big kitchen window. *Our patients
are like the leaves,* she says, spooning fresh grounds,

refilling the percolator. So we have that talk again.
Why some hold on so long and others just let go.

III

To see and know a place is a contemplative act.

—Gretel Ehrlich

After Driving Cattle in the Flint Hills

Tallgrass tangled in stirrups.
Cowhands leaning on long shadows.
After all these years,
I am still in love.

Elegy for a Prairie Town: Reflections on a Shallow Map of the Flint Hills

Since you moved away
the tame edges

of our hometown
have grown wild.

For years we propped up
what remained—

our old place, the barn,
even the schoolhouse.

Now, we are going away.
Think of our garden.

There was no need for windows
or doors. A long time from now,

even this absence will be forgotten.

Spring Matrix

We kept watch in the calving barn
until the pairs were safe in pasture.
Days later, after a hard rain,
we resumed our search of repose
below the limestone outcrop, turning
broken layers of ancient seabed,
scratching the rocks' underbellies
with our fingers, uncovering fossils
of floaters and swimmers, the matrix
of old life. We circled home, through
the pasture where heifers grazed freshened
buffalo grass—first calves at side,
the sounds of suckling and fragrance
of lathered milk. After supper,
on the west porch, Val lifted her drink
to the horizon—rain clouds holding
the sun's last light—and saw a fleck
of earth wedged at the edge of a nail
bed. She moved her hand for me to see.
The alfalfa will flower soon, she said,
and we'll be cutting hay.

It Was the Wind

Kansas Flint Hills, 1938

Winter whiteout rattled her windows, slipped beneath
doors and frosted wood floors, smothered fence
· posts and a side of the barn. Cattle and the dogs,
frozen in drifts.

Spring twister stripped shingles, ripped clapboards
and launched the barn like an ark into Wabaunsee County.
Hail shredded the cornfield
and her garden.

All summer southwind bent the landscape. An empty
sky sucked everything dry. The windmill, frantic
for water, pumped air, and home
overflowed with waves of dirt.

In fall, cool gusts scattered black walnuts.
She picked the nutmeats, then scrubbed
at husk-stained hands through another winter—
another snow melt.

Prairie Towers

slender mantises
seize wind
stir stratus soup
tumble butterflies
& feathers across
flatlands & foothills
feed electric grids
light the night

Flint Hills Patriarch

Before cattle drank from the Neosho,
when bison angled trails from water
to water & Kanza were people of the land,
this solitary Elm suckled from our spring's seep.

Years passed. Southwind's weight inclined
the great trunk, wrestled limbs northward
and fixed its branches as a half-open fist.
The tough old tree battled to a standoff.

It is said the lightning strike in 1955 stripped
bark from the trunk's southwest quadrant
baring cambium, hard and black
and cured the tree of Dutch elm disease.

The Work of Turkey Vultures

Under the tough old stars—
In the shadow of bluffs
—Gary Snyder

Prairie artisans sail from their roost,
muted flights to ride the morning thermal—
that long-winged ritual of tilting and
wheeling, searching for dead and dying.

There will be no anointing. No Last Rites.
Dissection and digestion is their craft—
transforming a carcass to vapor and dust.
The real work, what is to be done.

Last Hunt

Two pheasants break from the road ditch—
a tough flush in the squall of snow.
The dog, Julip, a quick breath behind,
startles a red-tail from an REA pole.
The hawk, a big female, stalls
in a wind gust, crashes across
an ice-glazed power line and tumbles
to the frozen switchgrass below.
I wrap her in my hunting coat,
unsheathe my knife and fashion a splint
from a shell casing. It's no use.
There are undeniable signs—
rhythms and beak claps,
sharp as castanets, mark time
with agonal gasps. A splinter of her wing
bone slices my hand. The clonic brush
of feathers against my coat paints the canvas
with our blood. At the end, tremors, and fibrillations—
felt not heard. I will bury her in the milo field
under the cottonwood we've plowed around
these years, where summers past she hunted
from the rustle of leaves, above my line of sight.

Great Blue Heron Forgets That Danger Comes from Above and I Forget She's Just a Bird

You, of all birds, forgot to look up! You should have learned
from your own tricks—sky plumage hovering over
the shallows of my stock pond, patient legs

masquerading as a pair of cattails, and your sudden
beak harpooning my baitfish, sunfish, black bass
and bullfrogs.

You're always punctual to waypoints—
from pond, to silo, to barn, to roost for the night—
you even sized me up that evening last March,

first time I saw you scull southwind with Olympian grace.
I saw your inquisitive eye when you cleared my barn.
I imagined that tilt of your head a signal for truce,

an invitation I accepted, raising my hand. You've kept
one eye inclined to the sky, against the red-tail's pillage
and the bald eagle's stoop. But not this evening, dammit.

I waved. I shouted, *Look up!* I watched your neck uncurl
and your legs extend, desperate to touch earth again,
and I saw that glance when you vanished

into the wall cloud's dark maw. I was helpless too.
All this has given me great pain. I imagined you
something you were not and couldn't save you.

Tide

The earth was forcing me to not forget her.
—Jim Harrison

My father believed the bedrock beneath our ranch—
    once an immense sea—
was still alive, that natural rhythms persisted
    in its sluggish consolidation.
He taught me to listen for echoes of breaking surf,
    but I couldn't hear them—
even at night with the wind quiet and my ear pressed
    to an outcropping.
He believed the gravitational pull of a full perigee
    moon could still move
the old limestone. He called it *land tide.* I thought
    that, too, improbable,
until one night the moon rose so full of light we could
    have counted the calves
in our pasture. Then, when its bottom edge caught
    the crest of a hill,
and just as I felt the prairie lift and inch sideways
    beneath my feet,
he said, *There. That's it.*

I have never recovered from that night, or the weight
of his hand on my shoulder.

Connections

Show me your environment
And I will tell you who you are.
—Boris Pasternak

We drive west for the Kansas prairie, my granddaughter and I—the one who talks with her fingertips and works in caves carved through tall buildings. *I want to understand what's to love about this place,* she says. *But please don't tell me what to think.* Near Alta Vista, we turn south on a gravel road then down a two-track that follows a section line into grass grown up her waist. She checks her cell phone and taps the screen. She's lost her connection.

We walk from the truck, leaning on the hard face of the wind. Our long shadows contract and expand with each swell of grass. She strokes at the seed heads like trying to stay afloat. When I stop to tell her we are passing over wheel ruts from an old wagon trail, she nods and moves on. When I explain the tops of these hills were set level by sediment from the Permian sea, she loops my arm in hers. *They need some trees to stop this wind,* she says.

So I lead her toward the creek called Jane's Fork, to shelter of old timber. Along the way I stop to touch the bluestems and Indian grass. A purple coneflower. *If you'll just learn the names,* I want to say. I pick an orange bloom from a butterfly milkweed—let it fall into her cupped hands. She turns it over with soft breaths, and I'm thinking . . . *and learn to paint the wildflowers.* We search a trail of chert washed free by spring rains. She finds a Munker's Creek point—tests its sharpness on a thumbnail. I want to tell her it's five thousand years old . . . *and she can learn pieces of our story from the artifacts.*

It will be dark soon. The wind has laid down. The brightest stars are burning through the veil of sunlight. I ask permission to tell a story—the myth of three constellations—Sagittarius the archer, aiming for Scorpio who aims to sting Orion hiding in the winter sky. I'll trace the trajectory from Sagittarius' bow to the scorpion's heart . . . *Just one false move*, I'll say. She laughs. She stays.

When Scorpio appears I wake her. I draw the sky-map. *You're right, she says, I can't see this many stars inside the city, but wind in town doesn't distort the landscape.* She draws the trajectory in reverse. *That arrow is still nocked. Don't you know? Everything moves at light-speed now.* I take her hand for the walk to the truck. No more talk. I'm careful driving the two-track in the dark, and just before it goes to gravel, I hear her tap her phone. Her signal has returned. She's searching for something at the speed of light, while I slow the truck even more, searching the limits of my headlamps for just one thing, in this prairie, she can love.

Reflecting on This Stone Wall

Conceived from stars in a Permian Sea,
born Trilobita and Pelecypoda
and cemented with their legion of dead,
these stones mortared our prairie's footings
for a quarter billion years until blasted,
quarried and vertically reassembled—
became this fence behind our barn,
our corral for springing heifers, a sun spa
for Texas horned lizards and one sultry
summer night, the cool bench, where long ago,
you and I first made love.

In Search of Place

For the listener . . .
nothing himself, beholds
Nothing that is not there and the nothing that is.
—Wallace Stevens

You come to the prairie searching for a way
out, constrained by agendas, contracts
and a sense you've missed something

more than a business opportunity. You're ready
to negotiate—slow the pace. You've nothing
to lose. Opting for a dirt road to a ranch

you'd heard about, you are astonished
by the nothingness, but you stay to see
it through. You borrow a 4 wheeler.

The rancher tosses you keys, points to wheel ruts,
says, *Follow the two-track to find your way.*
You leave your iPhone in the drink holder,

think to lock the car—then reconsider.
You ride to the crown of a hill, cut the engine
and wade into bluestem as tall as your waist.

You search after the soaring red-tail's scream
and consider your next move.

Crow Speaks His Mind After News of *Shock and Awe*

Let me lie here and dream of a better life . . .
Let me stay here with these birds
and listen to their rough songs.
—Brian Turner

Crow ascends from the corner hedge
as if the southwind will lift him above
all creation, then, in his usual way, suspends
over my gap gate crossing the two-track

to summer pasture. He's made a habit of hanging
around, watching me open this gate.
I consider Crow from my pickup—
windows down, radio full blast. He hovers

through the weather forecast and a seed corn
commercial, but, at the top of the hour,
with news of the aerial assault, he knows
we're at it again, and with a caw like a wail,

sails over rim rock to the bluestem below,
where his ancestors wept over our bloody
prairie incursion—where today
he will pretend we've never walked.

Sunset at Lower Fox Creek School

If you watch a sunset from beginning until the end—
it will change your life.
                    —Jim Harrison

A sunset can change your life. I say this as a promise. *There's more to a sunset than the watching.* The boy hesitates—the start of a grin. He kicks at debris from an old stone wall and startles a Texas horned lizard. He captures it under his ball cap. He turns it belly up, front legs paddling air, back legs absent. *Something bit it,* he says. *You take it.* I trace its serrated flanks one side to the other, confirming the symmetrical absence of hind legs and tail. *It was born this way,* I say. *A birth defect.* He releases it on the soft nap of buffalo grass and it paddles through a crevice into the rubble. *It made it without back legs,* he says. *It's a survivor.*

We slide between strands of barbed-wire fence. He wades through the ungrazed bluestem, arms raised like wings, clipping the tops of ripe seed heads until we come to a ledge of limestone. *Good place to sit,* I say. *Let's listen while we wait.*

I want him to hear the bobwhite whistling from sumac along the south draw. He squeals, imitating steel wheels scouring steel rails— the train that trembles our hill from the Santa Fe tracks to the south. I want him to say something like, *Do you hear that? Grasshoppers are crackling to a safe place for the night.* But he describes a sound like a kitchen blender—the Cessna 210 tracking across the west sky on course for a Wichita airport. Nighthawks strafe us, boom and buzz us like miniature spitfires. He asks if I think the whines of off-road treads against asphalt on Highway 177 come from American or Japanese tires.

When the sun hesitates—that point of descent where I worry it will drop out of sight if I look away—I squint against the light to hold a finger under its bottom edge. It's moving again—quick to the horizon. Darkness seeps into swales and gullies like rivers filling with black ink. Shadows of cattle lengthen, like loosening string ties. A northern harrier tightens its course to the quail's call, swoops into the sumac and, for a time, there is no sound at all.

It's dark when I hear the pulsing—the familiar *Thap. Thap. Thap.* The boy tugs my shirt, points to strobe lights in the south sky. *On course for Fort Riley,* I say. *It's a Huey. Could be an old med-evac from Vietnam. We called them dustoffs.*

The Huey swoops over us. Grass swirls and flattens to earth. Strobes flash blood and white phosphorous. Rotors slap my ears. I'm snugging tourniquets and starting IVs. A 105 shell rigged on the road to Phước Vĩnh. A rifle squad—most of them wasted. Unzipping and zipping and thuds of body bags stowed side-by-side. We've salvaged three, but two boots and an arm are bagged with the dead. The dustoff lands and we're starting to load when the boy grips my arm. *Hey Grandpa. The helicopter's gone.*

There is a sprinkling of light on the north horizon. I listen for the sound of rotors, but the wind has blown them away. *The best part was the lizard,* he says, still holding. *Yes,* I say. *The lizard. That meant the most to me, too.*

Afterword

Who, exactly, needs to read this book? The veteran whose memory is haunted by grim reminders of battle, who may be comforted to know that someone else remembers and understands; the young, who may harbor false, romantic notions of war as somehow glorious; the old, who may have forgotten the nature of battle and find it too easy to contemplate sending young troops out to new battlefields; those of us who have never experienced warfare, who need to grasp the ungilded reality of sudden death, irreparable wounds, enduring damage to body and soul, even—especially—to those who return alive. In fact, I can't think of anyone who doesn't need these poems, in this age of distant wars that touch us, the civilian population, only via electronic media and printed commentary.

As the widow of a World War II veteran, I recognize the narratives conveyed in these compelling poems: they recall incidents my late husband finally—reluctantly—learned to share with me and with our children, complete with unidentifiable body parts, the death of real buddies with names and families, encounters with the enemy that remain in the memory—and the nightmares—for a lifetime, whether as threats or as reminders of our common humanity and vulnerability, which war wants us to forget.

But there is so much more to this book, so much that anchors it in the universals of human experience outside of war, adding to its weight as lived history and its value as literature. There are civilians who wait and hope, go on with life after unspeakable losses, and themselves die. There are memories of a prairie childhood—the poet's—that speak for the sweetness of life, the magnitude of the sacrifice made by those who don't return. There are children and grandchildren whose presence broadens the focus of the book out to the future, raising questions about that future and our impact on it, and hinting at tentative promises.

H. C. Palmer has packed into this slender volume both the cost of war and the boundless beauty of peace on earth. Here is "After Driving Cattle in the Flint Hills," in its entirety:

> *Tallgrass tangled in stirrups.*
> *Cowhands leaning on long shadows.*
> *After all these years,*
> *I am still in love.*

So should we all be.

—Rhina P. Espaillat

Notes

If I Die in a Combat Zone is Tim O'Brien's first novel about the Vietnam War.

A Season for War: Billy's name is on *The Wall*, Panel 11 E, Line 63.

Resurrection: "America failed Sergeant Bales." Anonymous. Fort Leavenworth Prison

Death of a Dead Person: Dancing eyes is a euphemistic term sometimes used to describe the pathological eye movements known as *nystagmus.*

Prior to a career in internal medicine, H. C. Palmer was a battalion surgeon in the American War in Vietnam. He has also been a cattle rancher. He founded and leads a writing program for veterans at the Writers Place in Kansas City, and his work has appeared in such journals as *New Letters, Ekphrasis, Narrative Magazine,* and *War, Literature, and the Arts. Feet of the Messenger* is his first book.

This book is composed in Minion Pro and Optima.

Minion Pro was designed by Robert Slimbach for Adobe Systems, based on late Renaissance typefaces.

When designing Optima, Hermann Zapf was influenced by classical Roman capitals and the lettering on headstones in Florence.

The names on the Vietnam Veterans Memorial in Washington, DC, are carved in Optima, which inspired its use here.